NINJA, GO!

Written by
Julia March

Editors Emma Grange, Himani Khatreja
Assistant Art Editor Akansha Jain
Senior Art Editor Jo Connor
DTP Designers Umesh Singh Rawat, Rajdeep Singh
Pre-Production Producer Siu Yin Chan
Pre-Production Manager Sunil Sharma
Producer Louise Daly
Managing Editors Simon Hugo, Chitra Subramanyam
Managing Art Editors Guy Harvey, Neha Ahuja
Art Director Lisa Lanzarini
Publisher Julie Ferris
Publishing Director Simon Beecroft

Reading Consultant Linda B. Gambrell, Ph.D

Dorling Kindersley would like to thank
Randi Sørensen, Paul Hansford, and Robert Stefan Ekblom
at the LEGO Group.

First published in the United States in 2015 by DK Publishing
345 Hudson Street, New York, New York 10014.

www.LEGO.com

www.dk.com

A WORLD OF IDEAS:
SEE ALL THERE IS TO KNOW

Contents

World of Ninjago

Welcome to Ninjago!
Five brave Ninja protect
this magical land.
Their names are Cole, Jay,
Kai, Zane, and Lloyd.

They are masters of a
martial art called Spinjitzu.
The Ninja possess powers
of the four Elements of Ninjago.
These are Earth, Lightning,
Fire, and Ice.

Ninja, No More

The Ninja are sad.

Zane went missing after

a battle with an enemy.

Where could Zane be?
The Ninja do not feel
like a team without him,
so they split up.

Kai

This red Ninja is
the Master of Fire.
He has a hot temper!
Now that the Ninja team
has split up, Kai works
as a show fighter.
He thrills the audience
with his acrobatic moves.

Jay

Skillful Jay is the
Master of Lightning.
This blue Ninja is super
fast and adventurous.
Now that the Ninja team
has split up, Jay works
as a game show host.
His jokes make the
audience laugh!

Cole

This black Ninja is
the Master of Earth.
He is very strong and calm.
Now that the Ninja team
has split up, Cole works
as a lumberjack.
Chopping down trees
keeps him busy.

Lloyd Garmadon

This green Ninja is the
Master of all Elements.
He is upset that the
team split up.
He does not want to
get another job.
Lloyd still wants to be
a Ninja more than anything!

Zane

Zane is the Ninja of Ice.

He is a quiet and serious robot.

The other Ninja think that

Zane has been destroyed,

but he has rebuilt himself.

Where has he gone?

Will he ever see

his friends again?

NINJA WEAPONS

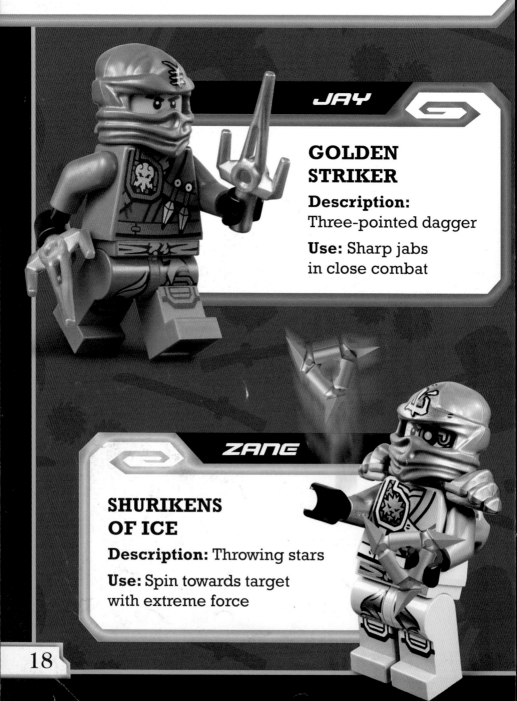

JAY

GOLDEN STRIKER

Description: Three-pointed dagger

Use: Sharp jabs in close combat

ZANE

SHURIKENS OF ICE

Description: Throwing stars

Use: Spin towards target with extreme force

COLE

STAFF OF THE DRAGONS

Description: Solid, long stick

Use: Strikes enemy and blocks attacks

KAI

GOLDEN KATANA

Description: Razor-sharp blade

Use: Cuts, slices, and defends enemy attacks

19

Sensei Wu

Sensei Wu is a wise
and good teacher.
He taught the Ninja
all of their skills.

Sensei Garmadon

Sensei Garmadon is
Sensei Wu's brother.
He used to be evil,
but now he is good.

NINJAGO TIMES

Volume 12

SENSEI GARMADON WRITES BOOK

Sensei Garmadon has written a book about his exciting life. We asked him to tell us more!

Can you tell us more about your transformation from bad to good?

I was a wicked dark lord. I told lies and even plotted to take over Ninjago! Now instead of fighting the Ninja, I spend my time training them.

REMEMBERING ZANE: New statue for much missed Ninja built in town center.

MYSTERIOUS POSTERS: Master Chen's followers put up posters in Ninjago. A special report.

Why did you change?

My son, Lloyd, and my brother, Wu, changed me with their goodness. I owe them my life.

Do you have a message for our readers?

I hope my story inspires other villains to give up their life of crime and live in harmony. Peace out!

Sensei Garmadon
An Autobiography

MY JOURNEY FROM EVIL TO GOOD

Master Chen

This villain is Master Chen.
He wants to turn people into
snakes called Anacondrai!
To do this, he must steal
the powers of the Ninja.
So he invites them to a
contest on his island.

Master Chen
presents:

THE TOURNAMENT OF ELEMENTS!

Are you the most powerful warrior in Ninjago?

Come to Master Chen's island to prove it!

BE THERE

(Bring this flyer for one free bowl of noodles)

Nya

Nya is Kai's younger sister.

She is very clever.

Nya thinks that the
tournament is a trap!

She follows the Ninja
to Master Chen's island.

She hopes she will find
Zane there, too.

TOURNAMENT ARENA

Welcome to Master Chen's tournament arena. The Ninja find that it is full of surprise obstacles. Enter at your own risk!

Swerve to sidestep the falling swords.

Dodge spinning blades!

Don't fall down the trapdoor leading to the fire prison!

SPINJITZU
Spinjitzu is an ancient form of martial art. A Master of Spinjitzu can spin so fast that he turns into a powerful tornado of energy.

Dash past poison dart missiles.

Watch out for this dangerous deck of daggers!

Skylor

Skylor is Chen's daughter.
She can steal the power
of any Ninja she touches.
Chen wants her to steal
the powers of the Ninja.
But when she meets Kai,
she wants to be friends
with them instead!

Clouse

Evil Clouse has a Book of Magic.
He uses a magic spell to help
Chen turn people into snakes.
It even works on Garmadon!

Pythor

Pythor has always been a snake.
Master Chen needs his help
to make Clouse's magic spell
last forever.

CHEN'S EVIL PLAN

Master Chen's follower, Eyezor, is devoted but dim. He is still confused about Chen's plan to defeat the Ninja and conquer Ninjago.

Anacondrai Army

Master Chen is now the leader
of a huge Anacondrai army!
He thinks nothing can stop
his plan to take over Ninjago.
But Sensei Garmadon still has
a good heart, even as a snake!
He uses a spell from the Book
of Magic to send Chen and
the Anacondrai far away.

Ninja Reunion

The Anacondrai are beaten!
Master Chen is gone for good.
But what really makes the Ninja
happy is seeing Zane again!

He was a prisoner on Chen's island, but now he is free. All five Ninja are back together. Where will their adventures take them next?

Quiz

1. Where do the Ninja live?

2. Which martial art have the Ninja mastered?

3. What does Kai work as after the Ninja split up?

4. Who is this Ninja in green?

5. What is Zane's element?

6. Where is Master Chen holding the Tournament of Elements?

7. Who is Lloyd's father?

8. Who is Nya's brother?

9. What power does Skylor have?

10. Who is this white and purple snake?

Answers on page 45

Glossary

Martial art   A form of fighting or self-defense

Acrobatic   Quick and flexible

Skillful   Having the ability to do something well

Autobiography   Book written by a person on the subject of his or her life

Tournament   A series of contests between a number of competitors

Obstacle   An object that blocks one's way

Reunion   Meeting up with a person or people after being separated for a period of time

Index

Answers to the quiz on pages 42 and 43:
1. Ninjago 2. Spinjitzu 3. Show fighter 4. Lloyd Garmadon
5. Ice 6. On his island 7. Sensei Garmadon 8. Kai
9. She can steal the Ninja's powers 10. Pythor

Guide for Parents

DK Readers is a four-level interactive reading adventure series for children, developing the habit of reading widely for both pleasure and information. These books have an exciting main narrative interspersed with a range of reading genres to suit your child's reading ability, as required by the Common Core State Standards. Each book is designed to develop your child's reading skills, fluency, grammar awareness, and comprehension in order to build confidence and engagement when reading.

Ready for a *Beginning to Read Alone* book
YOUR CHILD SHOULD

- be able to read many words without needing to stop and break them down into sound parts.
- read smoothly, in phrases and with expression. By this level, your child will be beginning to read silently.
- self-correct when a word or sentence doesn't sound right.

A Valuable and Shared Reading Experience

For some children, text reading, particularly non-fiction, requires much effort, but adult participation can make this both fun and easier. So here are a few tips on how to use this book with your child.

TIP 1 Check out the contents together before your child begins:

- Invite your child to check the blurb, contents page, and layout of the book and comment on it.
- Ask your child to make predictions about the story.
- Talk about the information your child might want to find out.

TIP 2 Encourage fluent and flexible reading:

- Support your child to read in fluent, expressive phrases, making full use of punctuation and thinking about the meaning.

- Help your child learn to read with expression by choosing a sentence to read aloud and demonstrating how to do this.

TIP 3 Indicators that your child is reading for meaning:

- Your child will be responding to the text if he/she is self-correcting and varying his/her voice.
- Your child will want to talk about what he/she is reading or is eager to turn the page to find out what will happen next.

TIP 4 Chat at the end of each chapter:

- Encourage your child to recall specific details after each chapter.
- Let your child pick out interesting words and discuss what they mean.
- Talk about what each of you found most interesting or most important.
- Ask questions about the text. These help to develop comprehension skills and awareness of the language used.

A FEW ADDITIONAL TIPS

- Read to your child regularly to demonstrate fluency, phrasing, and expression; to find out or check information; and for sharing enjoyment.
- Encourage your child to reread favorite texts to increase reading confidence and fluency.
- Check that your child is reading a range of different types of material, such as poems, jokes, and following instructions.

- Series consultant, **Dr. Linda Gambrell**, Distinguished Professor of Education at Clemson University, has served as President of the National Reading Conference, the College Reading Association, and the International Reading Association. She is also reading consultant for the **DK Adventures.**

Have you read these other great books from DK?

BEGINNING TO READ ALONE

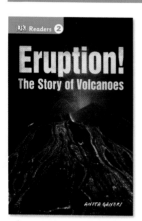

What spits out fire and ash? Find out all about volcanoes.

The Inquisitor is coming. Now there is no safe place for the Jedi to hide!

There are villains on the rampage! Who will keep the world safe?

READING ALONE

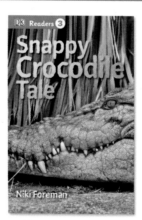

Join David on an amazing trip to meet elephants in Asia and Africa.

Follow Chris Croc's adventures from a baby to king of the river.

Discover the new tribes threatening Chima™ with their icy powers.